OVER
THE BRIDGE

Memories of a Leatherhead Lad from both sides of the Bridge

Brian Hennegan

ISBN 978-0-9552785-4-9

Published by:
Leatherhead and District Local History Society
64 Church Street
Leatherhead
KT22 8DP

Front Cover: The Bridge, Kingston Road, Leatherhead

Contents

Author's Note

This book has been written as a result of certain friends saying "you should write a book". So the following reminiscences are the result of me obeying the last instruction, as they say.

In the course of putting these few words together I have spoken to a number of people and was rather gratified to learn that my recollections coincided with most of theirs, but not necessarily in the same order, as Eric Morecambe would have said.

I must single out my very good friend Goff Powell. We are of the same vintage and spent our formative years living almost next door to each other. He has generously provided me with most of the pictures, together with helpful advice. I have been unable to trace some of the other photographers names or various copyright holders of certain material used in the publication. Please accept my grateful thanks. He would also chivvy me along, saying "how's the book coming on". In the end I had no option but to finish it.

My thanks go to Martin Warwick for his patient help and guidance. Without him the contents might not have seen the light of day.

Last and by no means least my thanks go to my wife Ros for her 'understanding'.

I hope the reader will find it to be of interest and that it will bring back many memories for those of you who are of a certain age. North Leatherhead, together with those other areas of my youth covered in the text, have changed almost beyond recognition.

I am grateful for all the help that I have received. However any errors and omissions are mine alone.

Today is tomorrow's history.

Brian Hennegan
Leatherhead 2009

Note: The illustration on the back page of the book is reproduced from the 1938 Ordnance Survey map with latter additions by kind permission of the Ordnance Survey.

INTRODUCTION

The title 'Over the Bridge' refers to the Kingston Road railway bridge and this modest treatise, tells the story of a childhood and early adulthood spent in North Leatherhead and covers a period between 1941 and 1956. Being a member of the North Leatherhead fraternity I and everybody else, would refer to South Leatherhead as being 'Over the Bridge' and I have it on good authority that some South Leatherhead folk referred to North Leatherhead likewise. The Bridge took on its own personality. Folk would say "crikey its hot, cold, wet, or the wind don't 'arf blow over that old Bridge". I trust that this explanation has now given you a taste of the local folklore.

The Bridge number attached to both parapets of the railway bridge on Kingston Road Leatherhead. Seventeen miles and Forty Seven chains from Waterloo. These replacement number plaques have recently been fixed to all bridges and culverts. Take a walk along the 'new' footpath from the bridge to the railway station and you can see that even the smallest drain culvert has been 'awarded' a new plaque.

Although the period covered is not that far back in time, it does of course portray much that is different from the present, with regards to personal attitudes and 'social culture'. Health and safety, as a formal philosophy, was a

A recent view under the bridge in Kingston Road, looking towards Ashtead.

long way into the future. As children and young people we had an immense amount of freedom. We really were able to wander the woods and the highways and byways, without the current fear, real or perceived, that every child was under threat of numerous tragedies. I and some friends cycled to Worthing, aged about eleven. (Of course I do realise that there were far fewer vehicles on the road then).

We also had 'double summer time'. The clocks were one hour ahead of GMT all year round and they were put forward a further hour during the summer months. This enabled essential war work to be performed in daylight, although it did make it difficult for young bodies to get to sleep. This arrangement ran from 1941 to 1947, but not in 1946. (What a quaint Nation we are). Most adults on the estate would look out for all the children. It would be no use at all for me to go home and say "Mrs Jones shouted at me and told me off". Mother would just say "I expect you deserved it". On the other hand if I had fallen over and grazed my knee, Mrs Jones could just as easily have washed and dressed it, and given me a cuddle. Mum would have been grateful. How very different from the possible reaction today.

In any exercise that looks back in time there is the ever-present 'bogeyman' of failing human memory. We all know how nature has a habit of bending and twisting our recollection of events. Indeed we are all aware that some 'definitive' historical accounts are guilty of repeating previously published inaccuracies. Of course the 'rose tinted glasses' syndrome can also provide a trap for most of us, but I truly hope that I have been able to subdue it. Nevertheless I can still name all the families living in Woodbridge Grove at the time and most of those living in Rye

This is an early view of Woodbridge Grove, Leatherhead, (c1930). Rye Brook Road is on the left of the photo.

Brook Road. The author's grandfather bought number 1, the house on the right hand side of the photograph, soon after it was built in 1926. It was here that the author lived during the period covered by this book. The houses were on the Council Estate but the first six houses, numbers 1-6, had been built for sale. There were approximately a total of 15 houses available for sale. Leatherhead Urban District Council was, obviously, ahead of the game in providing 'public and private' housing. At the end of the road, beyond the pile of rubble, you might just be able to see the brick wall that we walked along as youngsters.

As I still have many good friends and acquaintances, who were bought up 'Over the Bridge' (on both sides), I realise that there may be a few who will question some aspects of my recollections. Nevertheless I hope that this account will give a taste of that happy bygone age, fast slipping into the dark void of time.

PROLOGUE

It was a fine summer's day. It could just as easily have been during the last days of World War II or the early days of peace.

The pitch was in fine fettle, the teams had been selected and the batting order had been established. By a strange coincidence the first man in usually happened to be the one who owned the bat!

The fielding side was directed by the bowler, who was usually the proud owner of the moth eaten tennis ball, (not always readily available in those cash strapped days!)

We found that the wicket never varied. The road surface of Woodbridge Grove or Rye Brook Road was always reliable even after a torrential down pour. The umpire, who was usually the oldest amongst us, had ensured that the wicket was set up in the correct place, the crease had been firmly chalked on the ground and the coat on the ground serving as the bowler's stump was placed at the requisite distance. There was no problem with such things as bails, because the Prewett's Dairy metal milk crate, which served as a wicket, didn't have any. During the 1940's, apart from the occasional shower, the sun always shone, or has the 'rose tinted glasses' syndrome begun to kick in?

The game was usually a low scoring affair. A ball over a garden was a six and out. Mind you there were one or two gardens where the elderly owners would not return the ball and the players usually left the field voicing their disgust at the action. The gardener responding with 'I will see your mothers'. He never did, a fact for which we were very grateful. I have to admit however that the ball would sometimes be found the next day in the gutter, the grumpy old chap having relented. Mind you, the offending gardener could just as easily have been a woman. Apparently we were not the only players to suffer from this annoying problem. I understood that 'Cricketers' on other estates, and even those on 'the other side' of the bridge experienced similar frustrations.

Chapter 1
A Shopping Spree

When I set out on this venture I was unsure how best to avoid presenting the reader with a jumble of reminiscences. Finally I decided that I would try and gather the contents into groups of like subjects, (but I do crave forgiveness, if at times there are some deviations from this intended plan).

Woodbridge Corner - the junction of the Kingston Road with the Oxshott Road: this view, dated 1910, shows the area prior to the building of Sandford's Garage. However the view, with the garage, was much the same in the 1940's. The shop that became Hutton's was (and the building is still there) on the extreme right hand side of the photograph, hidden by the tree. Even back then an advertising board for R Whites mineral water was in place. The building in the centre background is the clubhouse of the Leatherhead Golf Club.

As they affected, and still affect, all members of the community it is appropriate to take a trip along the Kingston Road, in and out of the local shops. The vast majority were located on the North side of the Kingston Road railway bridge.

We will begin our trip at the extreme North end of Kingston Road. Just to the North of the Rye Brook was Mrs Hutton's confectionery shop and tea room (recently occupied by A1 Motor accessories, and now at the time of writing by Get Geared Motorcycle accessories). I have subsequently learnt that she was a 'Miss' and her name was Gertrude.

Her shop was frequented by all the local youngsters. The windows were covered in the moulded letters advising customers that the shop sold Fry's and Rowntree's chocolates. Inside the shelves groaned with large glass jars containing a large assortment of sweets, ranging from gobstoppers to a variety of boiled sweets and all types in between. I remember when I was out with my Grandad he could always be relied upon to produce boiled sweets from his trouser pocket duly covered in fluff. On entering Hutton's shop there was a wooden 'L' shaped counter on which stood an old National Cash Register. Arranged in front of the counter was an assortment of large square biscuit tins containing Crawford's Cream Crackers, Huntley and Palmer's assortments, and others including Smith's Crisps in the transparent bags with the blue salt bag. (The modern crisps do not taste the same, even allowing for the change in one's taste buds). Of course we must not forget the cat who would just sit anywhere he fancied. Did they really taste better than the current offerings, or is it just that our taste buds have 'deteriorated'?

In this view we can see Mrs Collin's shop. Butt's the grocers can be seen on the extreme right. The entrance to the future Council house estate will be made at the end of the terrace. In more recent times the terrace was demolished and replaced by flats. Two shops have been included in the new development.

Walking up the road in the direction of the bridge, the next establishment was Mrs Collin's shop. This was very similar to Hutton's. As most people walked in those days, both establishments served their own regulars. The same range of goodies were advertised in the windows. Bottles of ginger beer in stone bottles and 'Tizer the appetizer' were favourites with us youngsters.

Next door was Butt's the grocers, with its own unique smell, being an assortment of freshly cut bacon, tea, coffee, and a host of products that all housewives would require to feed her family. They would of course make sure that they had their ration books with them and Mr Butt or an assistant would cut the appropriate number of coupons from it with a small pair of scissors kept on hand for the purpose. Customers could place their orders using their own order books and if required the order would be delivered to their door by a delivery boy using the ubiquitous tradesman's bike with its wicker basket firmly placed in the front carrier. At least two of the author's friends performed this task at different times. Both Collin's and Butt's stood where the entrance to Rylands Court is now located. The Sandes Place and Aperdele Road Council Estate was not built until 1948.

If we cross the road, to where the veterinary surgery is now, we find Buckland's the Greengrocer. Here all the produce was fresh. Mr 'Snowy' Buckland went up to the old Covent Garden each morning in his van to get his produce. Nothing in his shop was vacuum wrapped or frozen. The spuds came with an amount of real dirt and nothing conformed to E.U. specification. Back in those halcyon days Europe took on a completely different interpretation. Occasionally 'Snowy' and his wife would have a disagreement and this would provide an interesting interlude for those customers brave enough to remain in the shop. Fortunately these bouts would soon pass and normal service would be resumed.

We stay on this (West) side of the road and after a short step we come to the 'Royal Oak' public house. Even this stalwart 'bench mark' has now taken on a different appearance today. In the period we are looking at there was no protruding frontage to the ground floor. Perhaps being a more 'local' establishment additional space was not yet required. There was no Clements Mead estate and where Leatherhead Glass Works now stands there was a late Victorian house that served as a roadside establishment under the name of 'The Willow Grange' café. This was run by members of the Chitty family, as we will shortly discover this was not the only establishment to have proprietors of that name.

I realise that I am deviating from shops but at the end of Lilliot's Lane (the narrow passage way running between the two timber cottages) stood a farm house with willow trees in the grounds. As one stood there the 'modern' world of the 1940's and 1950's felt very far removed. The owner kept two very 'enthusiastic' Alsatian dogs and when the author was delivering the family meat from the Co-op he would not venture within fifty yards of the place unless the working dogs were firmly secured in the house. Even then the

windows would rattle when they both expressed their 'delight in seeing me'.

Here Mr George Dench was the lord of all he surveyed. In the 1940's and early 50's the left hand bay of the building, including the first floor, was not there. In its place there was an entrance to the yard at the rear of the shop.

Where to now? We cross back over the road and we find the long established firm of Godwin and Shiels, they were ironmongers and builders. One could purchase almost anything from their shop. Door locks, gate hinges, nails of all dimensions, tyres and inner tubes for your bicycle, including the necessary puncture repair kit, packets of seeds, fireworks (only near to Guy Fawkes Day), air guns and rifles, clothes lines, hemp not plastic. The list is almost inexhaustible. The shop was managed and controlled by one George Dench, who was a well known personality and still fondly remembered by many. He passed away in 2001 and was a member of the Parish Church Choir for over eighty seven years, possibly a world record - his length of service with the Choir is legendary. Of course us youngsters and most of the adults, would only have known him as Mr Dench. As well as being the Manager of Godwin & Shiel he was well known in Leatherhead for his work with Toc H.

George Dench

Adults at that time would not easily resort to using Christian names. I spent many of my summer holidays with my Aunt Mabel in Hampshire and I recall that although she and her neighbour had lived next door to each other for many years, the greeting would always be, "good morning Mrs Woods" and "good morning Mrs Tomes". Such were the social graces that once existed.

We continue our walk along the road until we come to Mr Jackson's Green Grocers and Post Office. This occupied two adjacent shops (now the home of the Mole Bridge Medical Centre). It was very much a family run business with Mr and Mrs Jackson serving the customers with their fresh vegetables and other close family members attending to the Post Office business. Like all traditional shops such as this there was a familiar smell from the vegetables and the sacks of bran that stood open on the wooden floor. I remember that there was no till or cash register, both Mr and Mrs Jackson had a fabric cash pouch tied at the front of their aprons and all the cash transactions were through these bags. The Post Office had a traditional wire grill across the counter that transacted the official business.

There were a host of public service notices posted on a board and in later years the picture of the dreaded Colorado Beetle appeared, together with action to be taken should one catch sight of these striped villains. A pin-on badge making us all aware that this was not a stripey friend, but dreaded enemy number one. The poster carried a similar message, instructing us to contact the local constabulary if 'public enemy number one' was located.

The next port of call is not actually a shop, it is a traditional tea stall, painted green, and complete with iron wheels, although it was many years since it had moved because the wheels were sunk well into the ground. It stood where the second entrance road into the Council Estate is now, next to the recreation ground, pre 1948 remember. In the main the stall was patronised by lorry drivers and the occasional motorist, not that there were many of those at the time.

A Sentinel steam wagon, similar to those that frequented the green tea stall.

The lorries were of great interest to us lads. Some were 'modern' Sentinal steam wagons, from a firm called Kay's of Horsham. They travelled between there and the gravel pits in the Chertsey area. (The author knows this with hindsight). They were like magnificent beasts of burden, who would produce a cacophony of fascinating noises, as well as depositing ash and cinders on the road, whilst they waited patiently for their drivers to finish their 'brew and a wad'.

Close by in the corner of the recreation ground one would, at times, hear the clanking of ropes on steel as the local youngsters ran round and round on the 'Giant Stride'. No school there as yet.

I will try to describe this item of amusement. Imagine a steel post some ten to twelve feet tall, at the top of which was a wheel about two foot or so in diameter, mounted horizontally and able to rotate. With me so far?

Attached to this wheel were four or five ropes that hung down to within about four feet from the ground, with two or three knots conveniently tied to act as hand holds. To enjoy the fun of this sophisticated piece of equipment find another three or four mates. Each grasps hold of a rope and you run

Although this picture shows a giant stride being used by our cousins on the other side of 'the pond' it does provide a taste of the activity. Ours was taller than this one, or were we just a little shorter?

hell for leather round the 'maypole' and when you have developed a good head of steam hang on tight and launch off into the air in unison. Don't let go or you could be rewarded with a crack on the head as you made contact with the tarmac surround. Ah well, you soon learnt not to let go whilst your feet were still airborne. Today it would be called a 'steep learning curve'.

Enough of this dangerous activity. We will cross over the road again. In case you are confused by all this crossing and re-crossing, we have arrived back on the West side of Kingston Road, opposite the recreation ground. We are now standing outside Mellor's Stores, possibly the largest grocers and general store on the road.

The shop was where the 'One Stop' shop, Chinese take away, and Indian

Restaurant, now stand. Mellor's was another of those establishments where the house-wife was able to obtain most of the items necessary to sustain the family home, and if spare cash was available, some luxuries also. As a small lad Mother had made sure that I understood the difference between 'needs' and 'wants', and even today my dear wife will remind me of the difference, because I still find it hard to leave a 'bargain' book on the shop shelf.

MELLOR'S STORES
GROCERS
LEATHERHEAD
For
Groceries and Provisions at Competitive Prices
Families waited on daily
A Trial Order Solicited
Phone: LEATHERHEAD 118

THERE ARE OTHERS BUT LOOK FOR
JORDANS
FISH & CHIPS — KINGSTON RD. LEATHERHEAD
THE BLACK & WHITE SHOP

MAYS TUCK SHOP
(Mrs. Alcoe)
CONFECTIONERY, TOBACCONIST
ICES AND MINERALS
205, KINGSTON ROAD,
LEATHERHEAD.
Telephone LEATHERHEAD 3500

PHONE LEATHERHEAD 2825.
T. C. JENKINS, COAL AND COKE MERCHANT
183, KINGSTON ROAD, LEATHERHEAD,
Town Agent: HULME & Co., CORNER HOUSE, HIGH STREET.

A. GRIFFIN & SON,
HIGH-CLASS REPAIRS
— AND FOOTWEAR —
Kingston Road, Leatherhead.
ESTABLISHED 1863.

ERIC A. COLLINS
Tobacconist & Confectioner
Extensive Stock of Best Known Brands
Minerals - Walls Ice Cream
236 KINGSTON ROAD,
LEATHERHEAD.
'Phone LEATHERHEAD 3500

We now come to May's Tuck Shop, now occupied by B@titude. This was another of those local stores, not very big, in fact it was rather small. Mrs Alcoe (nee Chitty), there is that name again, was a purveyor of all things now known to be bad for the cholesterol. Sweets, chocolates, Tizer, Cherryade and of course ginger beer in the ubiquitous stone bottles. Ginger beer doesn't taste the same in glass bottles, or is there just a hint of those 'rose tinted spectacles' rearing their head again.

Next door to May's was Berry's. This was a haberdashery store, not as large as Wakefield's in the High Street, but nevertheless one could purchase most of the items required to make and repair clothing and household linen. As a small lad the author would accompany his mother to Berry's when she required further items for her dressmaking. I remember all the small wooden drawers containing items such as cottons, lace, pins and many things that a mere male could not comprehend. The shop is now a Bookmakers. Mother patronised Berry's to save money, now the punters frequent the establishment to lose money! Ah well that's progress for you.

We now pass the entrance of the small industrial estate and find Mrs Hersey's

Although this view was taken in the early years of the last century the picture would have been almost unchanged up until the 1960's. Mellor's store was the double fronted shop in the centre of the picture. May's Tuck Shop occupied the centre area and Berry's haberdashery was on the left. Berry's later became Jordan's Fish and Chip shop.

small shop. This was just an extended front room. The shop is no longer there but you can still see where it was. Number 197 with the protruding front window marks the spot. The shop door was to the left of the window. The interior had wainscot covering the lower half of the walls and most items seemed to be covered in a layer of 'clean' dust, Mrs Hersey sold cigarettes, Will's Woodbines, and Player's Weights predominated. These could also be bought in packs of five. She also sold tobacco, the ubiquitous Tizer, Monkey Nuts and a product we lads called 'Spanish Wood'. This was a woody liquorice substance which made your teeth black. We used to

A Bag of Spanish Wood

love chewing the small 'wooden' sticks. Looking back the very thought of this activity now fills me with something approaching disgust. However when you are young anything that costs one old penny and can be eaten was more than a fair temptation.

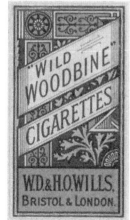

Plus your ten 'coffin nails'

We are almost at the end of our shopping trip along the road, and the penultimate search takes us to the corner of Dilston Road, where the tile shop is now. Back in the 'good old days' this was the establishment of Jenkins the coal merchant. In their window there stood the most beautiful model of a coal truck complete with their company name and standing on a length of railway line. (Well as a lad I thought it was beautiful). In those days they would take their lorry up to the railway goods yard and load up from the coal trucks that had been dropped off by the overnight goods train, steam hauled of course. Remember up until 1948 this would have been operated by The Southern Railway. On rare occasions I did visit the shop with my Grandad, when he placed a further order for coal, to 'keep the home fires burning'.

We now come to the last shop in the road, 'over the bridge on the north side'. This was Mr Griffin's boot repairers. Apart from repairing boots and shoes he also sold laces, stick-on soles together with the rubber fixing solution and metal studs, ideal for us lads to slide all along the ground and produce a shower of sparks. I do recall that the shop was filled with an aroma of freshly worked leather. Mr Griffin played a very prominent role in the running of the Leatherhead Football Club known as 'The Tanners'.

Well that concludes our shopping spree along the Kingston Road in that bygone age. I hope that each of you found some suitable item to purchase and if they have been bought at 1940/1950 prices so much the better.

Chapter 2

Dark Days and Light Interludes

I thought it would be appropriate at this juncture to take a look at the war years. I hasten to add that although I was a very young chap during the conflict, there are, nevertheless a number of events that have left an indelible impression on me.

Behind our garden in Woodbridge Grove there were fields and to the North the Ashtead Woods came right down to the Ryebrook. It was not until much later that they were extended back up the hill to their present boundary. During the war these fields were 'under the plough'. The fields and if I remember correctly there were four, were planted out with cereals of one kind or another. At harvest time the crop would be cut, using a binder pulled by a Fordson tractor. This operation required two men, or Land Girls, one to drive the tractor and one to sit on the binder. These binders with their large paddle arms, turning to sweep the crop into the cutting blades, were once a common sight, but apart from specialised use such as harvesting thatching materials, they have now been consigned to the annals of history. The binder would make its way round the field getting ever closer to the centre and you would hear the shot-guns firing as the rabbits ran from their ever decreasing cover. Well, rabbit was a good way to augment the food ration. Grandad was a 'man of means' and I had a lot of rabbit at that time. I have never knowingly eaten it since.

The binder bound the crop into sheaves and deposited them onto the ground. It was then necessary to gather them into stooks, each consisting of eight sheaves. These stooks would be built on a North and South alignment so that they would dry out, before being removed into a barn or built up as ricks. This was very labour intensive and required additional manpower. To provide this in our area, patients from the Epsom Asylums would be drafted in to help. Yes I am aware that this is a long outdated word but back then that was the accepted description of those establishments. The patients would arrive from Epsom in the back of an open top lorry. They were organised by a foreman and I still remember that his name was Mr Self. I also remember that Grandad allowed them to obtain water from the house. This was usually collected in a container by a swarthy skinned man who went by the name of 'Tojo'. If this harvest work coincided with weekends or school holidays, us lads, and lasses, would be allowed to help. If I concentrate hard I can still feel the scratches, feel the bites and smell the aroma of the freshly cut crop.

Away from the rural scenes there are many reminders of the war all around us. Although I was too young to remember much about the 'Battle of Britain', I do have vivid recollections of the later war years. Whilst standing in the front door porch with my Grandma we watched two aircraft (alas I do not know what type they were) trying to shoot down a barrage balloon that had broken away from its mooring cable. I remember asking my Grandad later "why hadn't it gone bang?". The answer "they were only lead bullets". Was there anything my Grandad didn't know?

As children we were issued with gas masks, as were the adults. I was the proud possessor of a bright red mask that had two round windows for eyes. It also had a floppy nose which would make a lovely rude 'raspberry' noise when you breathed out. Later, as I became a 'big boy', I was issued with a smaller edition of the adults mask which had a large rectangular window and no rude floppy nose. Why couldn't the adults have been issued with the 'Mickey Mouse' version? Obviously it would not have sat well with the stiff upper lip.

My wife Rosalie, who lived 'Over The Bridge', on the south side, relates the story that they only had one gas mask between three of them. They used torn up newspaper as toilet paper, so they used the box as a handy dispenser. No doubt a case of 'all for one, and one for all'.

I was born in Essex, yes, I am an 'Essex Boy'. Mum was a school teacher and had taught in Wickford and on Canvey island. She also taught in Wandsworth and Raynes Park before she and Dad had moved to Thundersley. When the 'Balloon went up' Dad joined up, and was to serve in Africa, Italy and other theatres of war, with the Royal Corp of Signals. Occasionally he came home on leave, but unfortunately like many children of my

The 'Mickey Mouse gas mask' which must have been issued to thousands of youngsters during the Second World War. By blowing through its nose a fantastic 'Whoopee Cushion' noise could be made. The one pictured here can be seen in The Leatherhead Museum, Church Street, Leatherhead.

age, Dad and I did not spend much 'quality time' together, during my early years. (I do detest that phrase 'quality time').

Mum and I moved up to Leatherhead to stay with my Grandad and Grandma in Woodbridge Grove. When we arrived in Surrey Mum was allocated a teaching post at Fetcham School. In those days the school was located in School Lane and apart from using the village hall and a wooden hut, that stood in the current hall car park as class rooms, this was the only accommodation for all children from five to eleven years old. The wooden hut also doubled as the school canteen. This entailed the incumbent class all moving up to one end of the hut fifteen minutes before lunch time, to enable the dinner ladies to lay the tables and prepare for the 'feeding frenzy'. When Mum took up the teaching post in Fetcham I was still too young to attend school officially, but apparently I was allowed to enrol at Fetcham. That's how I came to spend my school time from the age of four to eleven in a 'foreign land' on the wrong side of the bridge.

What has this got to do with the war? During my time at Fetcham we had a number of air raid warnings, signalled by the wailing of the siren. These air raid sirens were placed at strategic locations and sang out their mournful message. The first warning was an up and down note that lasted for a number of minutes. When the raid had passed the 'all clear' was sounded, as a continuous level note.

At the first warning we all had to go quickly, but in an orderly manner, into the air-raid shelters. There were four of these shelters, at Fetcham School,

'Moaning Minnie' - Wartime
air raid siren

three of which were arranged along the top edge of the school playing field alongside The Street, and one at right angles alongside the garden of the bungalow opposite the Village Hall. These shelters were constructed of concrete and buried under a generous mound of earth. Access was gained by a small flight of approximately eight steps. There was an escape hatch in the roof at the opposite end to the entrance. The actual shelter area consisted of a long narrow corridor. There were duckboards on a floor, which was usually damp. Running along each of the walls there were continuous wooden slatted benches. At the far end of this corridor was the toilet area containing a chemical W.C. This was made 'private' by a Hessian curtain hung from the ceiling. Looking back in retrospect I expect that it was one of Henry Moore's corn sacks. Those of you who have spent any time for real in one of these shelters, will no doubt still be able to conjure up the smell of dank, damp concrete, together with the other odours from the 'private' place. Did our education suffer as a result of these disturbances? Not on your life. We sang our multiplication tables until we were 'word perfect'. Sometimes when aircraft were heard overhead the teacher in charge would lead us in some sophisticated choral work entitled either: Ten Green Bottles or One Man Went to Mow. It did take me some time however to decode the meaning of 'Maisy Dotes and Dosey Dotes'.

We used to travel to Fetcham on the 462 bus. One bus went through to Staines, whilst each alternate one did a round trip to Fetcham only. It went up School Lane, along The Street, turning into Cobham Road and laying over at Orchard Close. Everyone referred to this service as 'The Swinger'. One morning Mum and I, having heard the air raid siren as we got off of the bus, ran into the Village Hall, were Mum

This photograph was probably taken somewhere in the Staines area. The T. Type vehicle is typical of the period. The 'running plates' cannot be clearly seen, but the vehicles servicing the route would have been provided by either Leatherhead or Addlestone garage

had her classroom and dived under the sturdy teacher's table. We had been there for a little while, when an Air Raid Warden came in and asked "what on earth are you doing?" Apparently we had heard the all clear. The 'Moaning Minnie' had gone off whilst we were on the bus. Mum was most embarrassed, but for years afterwards she would say to family and friends "Have I told you about the time when Brian and I dived under the teacher's table in Fetcham Village hall?" Of course the dutiful response would be, "No Alice you haven't".

As we are still on the wrong side of the bridge, we will spend a little more time with the 462 bus. During the war some commercial vehicles and a small

This rather fuzzy photo shows a 462 bus towing a Producer Gas Trailer. Note the Anti-Blast netting on the bus windows

number of buses, ran on what was known as producer gas.

This was an ingenious system requiring a vehicle to tow a small two wheel contraption containing a slow fire that gave off a gas that was taken into the engine in place of the usual petrol/air mixture. Leatherhead Bus Garage had buses that worked on this system and for some years after the war the anthracite store stood in the garage yard next to where the 65 bus used to lay over, before returning to Ealing - Argyle Road, or Turnham Green. (Prompting some of us smart Alec's to ask the driver "where was his paint tin?")

The gas system was only suitable for journeys over a fairly flat route and the 462 was worked by this system for a short time. I can remember kneeling on the back seat of the bus and watching this trailer bumping up and down and seeing the condensing water bubbling in the top of the combustion chamber. Can you imagine this being allowed in today's health and safety environment. Imagine a public service vehicle full of people, towing a two wheeled trailer full of fire with hot water being scattered on the road. I don't think so.

The development of these producer units is of local historical interest. During the war the late lamented firm of Neil and Spencer Ltd., were involved in the development of this technology. Two London Transport STL Type double deck buses had been licensed to them for experimental use. At that time the

Company was located in premises next to Effingham crossroads.

During the war many Canadian troops were based in the area. At Fetcham some of these troops were billeted in The Lodge located on The Street. One Christmas, forgive me I can't remember the year, it must have been 1943 or 1944, these Canadians gave a party in The Lodge for the Fetcham School children. We were given a whale of a time. We had a film show featuring all the favourite cartoon characters, Mickey Mouse, Donald Duck, Goofy and others. The food was out of this world. Remember the Country was in the grip of rationing. We had things we had not seen before. As youngsters we obviously had no knowledge of a world prior to the war. Jelly, Ice Cream, Gooey cakes, Sticky buns, Trifle, even fruit, seemed to arrive in a never ending procession. Each child left with a present. I have since learnt from Mum that many children had a severe bout of 'Jippy Tummy' and that I was a little bit sick. Since then Canadians have been A1 people with me.

Well, we have spent too long in Fetcham. Come with me to the Bus Garage, where we will jump on the 65 and make our way back 'Over the Bridge'. But before we do I must just relate an activity that has now passed into the history books, unless of course you frequent county fairs. Sometimes, coming home from Fetcham School, I would spend my bus fare on doughnuts from Maples shop in Cannon Grove, Fetcham. This meant that 'shanks pony' had to be employed.

Mizens were the owners of the watercress beds in Cobham Road, Fetcham and they also farmed the adjacent fields. Here if you were lucky you could see Mr Holland ploughing with the help of the two magnificent shire horses called Captain and Major. I can see them now slowly and purposefully plodding across the field with Mr Holland guiding the plough. Just a quiet word from him would give them their next move, but I expect Captain and Major knew how the game was played, possibly better than Mr Holland. Incidentally Mr Holland lived at the top end of Woodbridge Avenue and he knew my Grandad. Now that's street cred!

Of course we can't leave my recollection of the war years without further mentioning the subject of air raid shelters. At home we had a shelter at the bottom of the garden. It consisted of a partially buried structure built of railway sleepers and covered with earth. Grandad worked on the Southern Railway so it was cheaper for him to use acquired railway sleepers, than to obtain an Anderson shelter. These structures were fabricated from corrugated iron and would be delivered in 'flat pack' form, although that description had not been coined back then.

The proud owner would have to get some lads, or lasses, round to dig a hole and assemble the shelter therein then cover the lot with the earth taken from the hole. Plant the mound with marrows or other flora and crawl inside when 'Moaning Minnie' went off.

I can remember spending time 'down the shelter'. The smell of tar from the railway sleepers seemed to get into bedding and clothes. Mum will sometimes take great delight in reminding me that in the early days of the war, I would look up through the top of the open stable type door and say "tars, tars". No, I was not referring to the smell, I could not pronounce my 'S'es' and was trying to say Stars.

Towards the end of the war we did get a 'Morrison' shelter which was erected

in the front room. These were very substantial table like structures, built from heavy angle iron sections which bolted together with movable stout wire 'walls', and a plate steel top. This alternative was far preferable to the 'dug out', which was quickly put to a more productive use.

Grandad was an old countryman and was very self-sufficient. He grew most of his own vegetables and had a huge allotment, of which more later. He also produced a variety of home-made

The Morrison shelter (or cage) was named after the government minister Herbert Morrison. As this picture shows it was constructed using heavy steel angle section, the purpose being to protect the occupants from falling debris.

wines. When the garden air raid shelter became vacant he used it to mature the wine in large earthenware pots sealed with a cork bung. During the maturing process he would take samples. This was done by inserting a length of red rubber hose pipe through the bung and removing the sample by siphoning the wine into the mouth for tasting. Of course I would be with my Grandad when this 'technical' operation was performed.

The Royal Corps of Signals.
They obviously intended to lay a large quantity of cable!
The author's Dad is second from right, on the second pile of cable drums.

A few days later I gathered some of my friends together, including my friend Goff Powell. We made our way to the shelter, which I had been forbidden to enter on pain of death. I knew how the siphoning ritual was performed. There were about four stone pots and before long there were four or five of us each sucking on the rubber hoses with great enthusiasm. Now, we all know now that sucking alcohol through a straw is not the best way to maintain a clear head. Needless to say in a very short time we were all 'out of it'. Of course the details of what followed are not clear to me. A group of youngsters emerged from the shelter very ill indeed. Mothers up and down the road were heard to mutter "how irresponsible to leave that stuff where youngsters could gain access". Mum has since related that my Grandma, who was at all times a gentle, quiet woman, 'bent' my Grandad's ears back through one hundred and eighty degrees. From then on the door to the shelter was firmly padlocked.

There were air raid shelters in the Kingston Road recreation ground, located on the south side alongside the school playground. These shelters were of the above ground brick variety, surmounted with a cast concrete roof. When you entered you had to do a 'dog leg' round an anti-blast wall. I never went in these during the war, but I have friends who did. Their observations were similar to mine at Fetcham, i.e. they were not the most pleasant places to be. I do have other memories of the wartime period, such as occasionally travelling with Mum back to the bungalow at Thundersley in Essex, via London. Trains would sometimes be diverted, and you could arrive at an unexpected destination. But that is another story.

Two last thoughts. I can still recall the prayer that I said each night with Mum; "Dear God, please take care of all the sailors, soldiers and airmen, and especially Daddy".

I can also remember asking Mum, "when the war is over will there still be any news on the wireless?" I can recall Mum replying "I expect they will find something to talk about dear". How right she was!

Chapter 3

Business and Places

Today there are far more business and trading establishments, north of the railway bridge, than existed in the 1940 and 1950 period. Nevertheless, for all that, those that did exist were varied and interesting.

Let us start at the extreme northern end of the territory. Up on the hill, behind where B&Q is now, stood the club house of the Leatherhead Golf Club painted white and for many years a prominent land mark, visible along the length of Kingston Road from the railway bridge. It was damaged during the war, repaired, and only finally succumbed when the M25 motorway was built in the early 1980's.

If we take the right hand fork at the 'Tesco' roundabout and travel up the hill, we will see, on the right, a gap between house numbers 328 and 330. The space at the back of these houses is now occupied by the properties in Ryebridge Close. Back then all this ground was occupied by Eddison's Road Construction Company and used as a park for their steamrollers, water bowsers and the drivers sleeping vans. The vast majority of their work took place in the summer months, just as the tar and gritting re-surfacing work does today.

Steam Rollers

During the winter all the rollers and a few traction engines would be parked up here. There would probably be close on fifteen to twenty engines in the compound, with canvas or sacking covers over their chimneys and tarpaulin drapes covering the driving area. Occasionally rollers would be taken to or from the yard by a low loader. Us lads never ventured in. The watchmen and their rampant dogs would make sure of that. I have it on good authority from my good friend Arthur Taylor that the yard was known, by the immediate locals, as 'Greenie's Yard', but I never knew it as such.

In the spring the sight of these monsters on the move was a sight to behold.

24

Each roller would leave the yard towing its wooden caravan, sometimes with the driver's wife and water bowser. Just like the TV film shots of dear old Fred Dibnah and his mechanical procession. With the roller chuffing and the iron wheels of the van and bowser grinding on the road surface, the sight, smell, and sounds were truly magnificent. A re-enactment of similar processions will draw a crowd at any county show. For us lads it was an accepted event. Ah happy days!

Alas, by the time this photo of Sandford's Garage was taken the pantile roofs, covering the petrol pumps, had been removed to enable larger vehicles to take on fuel The Kingston Road running up the hill is in the foreground and the Oxshott Road is in the top left hand corner.

We will now come back down the hill to the 'Tesco' roundabout. In the fork formed by the Oxshott Road and the Kingston Road, stood Sandfords Garage. This was a very handsome structure. It had some 'Art Deco' features. The petrol pumps were arranged in two batches. One to serve the Oxshott Road, and the other to attend to the needs of those travelling on Kingston Road. The pumps can be seen in the picture, left of centre, by the corner of the building. The architect could not allow the motorist to stand out in the open, so each pump complex was covered by a shelter, but this was no simple affair. Each shelter was attached to the main building and supported by two pillars of a pleasing design. The roofs were clad with beautiful green glossy pantiles. This was unusual at the time it was built, because in those days most garage petrol pumps would not be under cover and if they were the shelter would more than likely be a very simple affair. The architect had not stopped there, because the top of the main building was surmounted by a weathervane, cut from thin gauge steel, depicting a period car

Sandford's Weathervane

25

being fuelled at a pump, complete with an attendant (it can now be seen in the Leatherhead Museum). Not only was there a large workshop area, but a substantial showroom was visible behind plate glass windows. At the rear there was parking and storage space. If the garage had managed to survive a little longer it might just have become a listed building.

Crossing over the Rye Brook bridge, which then had brick parapets capped by shiny bull-nose engineering bricks, we find on our left (travelling towards the railway bridge) the builder's yard belonging to Mr A G Nunn. This area served his needs in the 1940's. As Mr Nunn later said to my Dad, "things were far less complicated then Eric".

When Dad returned from the war he spent a short time with Mr Nunn, on a part time basis, sorting out the company paperwork.

Next door to the builder's yard there was, and still is, the large double fronted house that was owned by Mr Law. He and his wife ran a taxi business. He later began a coach hire operation, and his Bedford OB Duple Vista bodied coach was a familiar sight in the area. He was later to sell this part of the business to H R Richmond of Epsom, better known today as Epsom Coaches and Quality Line Buses.

This was not the only string to Mr Law's bow. He kept pigs at the rear of his property and the

noise at feeding time had to be heard to be believed. Today the neighbours would have kicked up a stink, pardon the pun, and the piggy wiggys would have been no more.

We now enter the Woodbridge estate and turn left into Rye Brook Road. On the left, where the road does a dog-leg we find the Surrey Saw Mills. The site is now occupied by numbers 1 to 15 Rye Brook Road. The mills were a continous hive of activity. Large tree trunks would come into the mill usually on a lumber wagon hauled by their Bedford O type articulated unit. I remember it was painted green, probably a colour well suited to a business involved with trees.

The sound of the circular saws transforming the trunks into timber bulks and planks could be heard all over the estate and surrounding areas. Once the timber had been processed it would leave the mill, either by their own transport or a contractors vehicle. Imagine a modern lumber wagon trying to negotiate those right angle corners today! The vehicles of yesteryear were much smaller and there would have been no parked cars to snarl up the exercise.

Of course the operation of cutting and planing produced huge quantities of sawdust and shavings. These would be snapped up by the locals for lining rabbit hutches, hamster cages and used as cat litter. The dry shavings could also help to start a bonfire when the gardening rubbish was damp and reluctant to do the decent thing. In the days before clean air was an issue an autumn evening could, at times, take on a 'misty' look. I believe that the mills later relocated in Farnham and retained the name Surrey Saw Mills. Still very appropriate as Farnham is just inside the Surrey Border.

Back on the Kingston Road on the right hand side stood Middleton's Laundry. Part of the site is now occupied by the Brook Way Industrial Estate.

You can see from the photograph on the next page that to the north of the buildings there was open ground stretching down to the Rye Brook. In the summer and during dry spring and autumn periods, this space would be a mass of drying garments, hanging on the clothes lines. I don't think that in 'today's culture' it would be a wise move to leave Mr Brown's shirts and Mrs Brown's drawers, on the line for the taking. I expect some items wandered even back in those 'good old days' but not sufficient quantity to bring the process to a halt.

The two detached houses in front of the laundry housed employees. During the period in question the one on the right was occupied by Mr. Watson, the laundry manager and the one on the left was the home of Mr. Kelleway, the van driver and caretaker. I used to take Mum's special items to the laundry with the order book. The items would be listed and priced in this book and returned with the counterfoil of the works ticket. When the garments were collected the cash would be handed over, the book would be receipted and you would take the clean washing home as a 'brown paper package tied up

with string'. That was the
easy bit. You still had to
get it home in the same
condition that it left the
laundry!

I can still conjure up the
smell of the laundry. It
was a mixture of steam,
soap and wet washing.
There was also the sound
of the machinery, the
hissing of steam and the
melodious tones of the
ladies singing the latest
'pop song'. (Did I hear
'Maisy Dotes and Dosey

Middleton's Laundry - This aerial shot was possibly taken in the 1930's. The two company houses are bottom left. The drying lawns can be seen to the right and the shadows of the clothes posts can be clearly seen. The Rye Brook is just out of shot in the bottom right hand corner.

Dotes', or am I letting my imagination get the better of me?)

Middleton's also had a laundry at Hook. It was just past the Ace of Spades roundabout, on the right hand side, behind the parade of shops. Although the building was not identical to the one in Kingston Road similar architectural features could be recognised.

During the war, Ronsons had a factory at 'Dorincourt', in Oaklawn Road, which was engaged in war work. The ladies who worked there were transported in one of Ronson's Fordson lorries that had wooden slat benches along both sides.

There was a canvas cover for use in wet weather. The lorry had a pickup stop at the entrance to the Woodbridge estate. The 'loading' procedure was simple. The driver would go to the rear of the vehicle and slide a set of wooden steps down and the ladies would clamber up holding on to a rope hanging from the centre of the cover frame. I can remember, as if it were yesterday, seeing the knotted head scarves and hearing the loud cheery greetings as the ladies joined their fellow 'passengers'. Although of course I didn't know it at the time, the driver was an old soldier who had lost part of a leg in the First War and was the great uncle of my future wife. Later I got to know him as Uncle George. He was a character.

Next to Middleton's Laundry were the premises of Nobles and Hoare. They were varnish manufacturers, and surprise, surprise, were always referred to as 'the paint factory'. On one occasion, part of the works caught fire, you can just imagine the consternation that caused.

Earlier we looked at Sandford's Garage and remarked upon its smart 'modern' appearance. On the site now occupied by Hardy Engineering, Mr Luff had his garage and workshop. This could be said to represent many such establishments up and down the country at that time. Not for Mr Luff a smart rank of petrol pumps. He dispensed fuel from a hand operated pump that delivered one gallon at a time and stood a little way up the entrance to the workshop. To reach the car that was to be fuelled, a hose fixed to an overhead arm, was swung out over the pavement.

There was of course plenty of head room for pedestrians, but if the hose was removed from the car in an 'enthusiastic manner' drips from the residue in the hose would drop on the ground. The Health and Safety Officials would have had a field day. Oil was also stored in forty gallon drums. On the top of the drum there was a hand pump and the oil would be pumped into pint or quart cans, for pouring into the appropriate engine orifice.

Mr Luff also ran a coach hire business, and Luff's Coaches were a well known sight. If my memory serves me correctly he had four or five vehicles. He catered for a variety of organisations, including Sunday Schools, Church groups, the Co-op social group and various sporting organisations. Theatre trips would also be on his itinerary and in those days before the advent of mass car ownership, we must not forget the inevitable trip to the seaside. Us lads spent many a happy hour going to the seaside in one of Mr Luff's coaches.

I well remember that everyone on the coach would sing all the way back from Littlehampton to Leatherhead. We all aquired a vast repertoire of songs, with the proper words, I hasten to add. On reflection it was rather like the air raid shelters, but in daylight, and on wheels. (By then of course, I had sussed out the Maisy Dotes and Dosey Dotes bit).

Chapter 4
Play and Leisure

I have already mentioned that as youngsters we had complete freedom to wander and roam at leisure, in a world of discovery and excitement. In those far off days we made our own amusement. Yes, I know that it is a well worn cliché, but it is nevertheless true for all that. We had no television, or computer games, with which to while away our time. As for mobile 'phones, well, in the 1940's and1950's only a minority of private residences were connected to the G.P.O. (General Post Office) telephone system and would rely on the red phone box. Us lads and lasses, would rarely pass an empty box without popping in to 'press button B', in the hope that the previous user had been unable to 'make a connection' and had omitted to press button B and retrieve their money, usually two or three old pence. If you were lucky, on the very rare occasion, you might hit the 'jackpot' and get six old pence, or a tanner, as it was always referred to. Don't laugh sixpence (2.5p) would buy you three bars of chocolate, or a small stone bottle of ginger beer, or a host of other 'rubbish' to put down your throat.

We spent hours in the woods. There were, and still are, two to choose from. The Ashtead woods to the North East of the Woodbridge estate and the Oxshott woods to the West. The Oxshott woods stretched from the 'Tesco' site to Oaklawn Road in the North and they ran along the Rye Brook to the West as far as fields off Randalls Road. In fact they ended at the site of 'The Mounts Manor House', a historic establishment. I saw the newly opened excavations in the late 1940's when our class from Fetcham School was taken there on a visit by the late Mr Snellgrove. His son John was a classmate of mine.

Back to the woods. Just by the bridge over the Rye Brook in Kingston Road, there stood a large Oak tree, of course at that time there was no Tesco and no Dobbes Nursery, which had preceded it. That tree was a fine climbing frame, however it lacked suitable branches nearer the ground so we made some steps by banging groups of six inch nails into the trunk, presto job done. You can see by this action we were not 'mindless vandals'. In the past there had been extensive brickworks in the woods and the remains of this activity was evident all over the place. There were the ponds that resulted from the clay excavation. There was an area that we knew as the rabbit warren, for obvious reasons. The rabbits must have found the broken soil, created by the brick debris, very suitable for their burrowing activities.

If the wind seemed to be favourable we would raid the cupboards for brown paper. Kites would be made, but unfortunately they tended to spend the whole of their existence wrapped around the few telephone wires on the estate.

Building camps absorbed a lot of our energy. They were similar to the sort of structures that Ray Mears creates for his 'Out Door' films, except that ours took an age to build and were not very waterproof. Never mind we would disappear all day, light a fire, bake spuds in the embers, fry eggs in an old frying pan and return home black as 'Newgate's Knocker' and probably smelling to high heaven!   I don't think our Mums were over anxious. The usual greeting was not "where have you been?" but "do you know what time it is?"

Just to illustrate a point, there was at one time, two chaps living in the Oxshott woods. They went by the name of Ted and Bill. We would visit them at their camps. Ted was a enterprising chap. He would make a type of hanging flower basket from wood. These he would line with moss and fill with flowers. He rode an old 'stop me and buy one' ice cream vending tricycle, and he would go into Leatherhead and sell the results of his labours.   I can't remember any of us being told "not to visit that old bloke in the woods". In fact Ted was called in by the local constabulary to assist in a murder hunt. A copy of the newspaper

The hermit in the woods at Oxshott

In the Seventies, a recluse lived in the woods between Oxshott and Leatherhead. "Old Ted" Churcher's home for more than 30 years was a tent in the wooded Pachesham Park next to Prince's Coverts.

Sometimes he could be seen wheeling a barrow along the Leatherhead Road, near The Star pub.

He proved to be a valuable help to police in 1971 when the Leatherhead Golf Course murder inquiry was launched, because his valuable knowledge of every nook and cranny of the countryside near Pachesham Gate, helped police find the body.

As you can see from the date in this cutting from the local paper, 'Old Ted' was around for some time.

cutting gives an account of the incident.

We also spent some time in the Ashtead woods. The main memory of these woods is the regular frequency with which they caught fire, resulting in a grand turnout of fire engines from the surrounding area, and no, we did not start the fires just to see the fire engines. I don't say we were never naughty, but we would not do a thing like that. On one occasion we were all returning back, rather late in the evening, from watching one of the fires when we met Mr Hayton, our next door neighbour and father of Roy. He had come to see where we had all got to. "Mr Hayton", I said, "you should see how big the fire is", he said to me, "if you don't run home quickly you'll get a fiery backside". Don't ask me what I had for dinner last night, but I can still remember that exchange almost verbatim.

At the bottom of Woodbridge Grove we find the Rye Brook. Before the days of Ryebridge Close, the North side of the brook was bounded by a wall made of glazed light yellow bricks. This ran from the bungalows standing in the 'First Slip' (the last unmade road up the hill behind B&Q) almost as far as the bridge by the now B&Q roundabout. It stood (and still stands in places) about ten feet high, and made a grand 'tight rope' to walk along. It formed the basis of many a 'dare'. It can still be seen at the bottom of Woodbridge Grove, at the entrance to Ryebridge Close. The brook was a grand place to play and we spent happy hours standing bare foot in the stream catching 'tiddlers' and making dams. It was, however, one place that our Mums were not too happy for us to be. Some time later one of our friends did fall right in and swallowed a quantity of water. He was extremely ill and from then on the attraction became less interesting, or was it because we were all growing up?

In 1947 R.D. Barton and Company began work on building the Sandes Place and Aperdele Road, Council Estate. As you can imagine this made a fine playground after work had finished in the summer evenings.

The scaffolding made superb climbing frames, until old Mr Thompson and his Dalmatian dog appeared on the scene. He would wave his stick and shout at us. I think the gist of his message was "why don't you young people go home to bed". At least I think that was what was being said!

Incidentally a pair of houses were completed prior to the rest of the estate being finished, I suspect that they were 'show houses' for the Council Officers to inspect. These houses are now numbered 34 and 36 Aperdele Road.

On Bank Holiday Mondays we would all troop along the Rye Brook in the direction of Randalls Road and make our way to the fields, now occupied by

Typical Grass Track Meeting

Unilever and Logica, in order to watch the grass track racing that was organised by The Leatherhead Motorcycle Club. The admission for us lads was very cheap because there were no ticket kiosks next to the hole in the fence.

The combined smell of cut grass, mixed with petrol, dope, and oil, was the perfect addition to those halcyon summer afternoons.

What else did we get up to? I have already mentioned the 'test matches' played in the road. Obviously football was another favourite game, however this was usually greeted by cries from the grown ups of "why don't you take that ball down to the Rec and play there". We usually did, not because of the pleas, but because there was obviously more room there for self expression. I was not a very good exponent of the art, but some of my mates were quite useful and played the game competitively for years.

Roller skating was another activity that tended to come round in its 'due season'. It was strange how all the games had their unwritten time of year, e.g. hoops, hopscotch, conkers, (not a pair of goggles, or crash helmet in sight,) plus many other activities.

Back to the roller skates. There were no skate parks so we tended to extemporise, (not a word I knew back then) so we skated down the middle of the Oxshott Road, in and out of the white lines in the centre. Dangerous, not on your life. We carried out a 'risk assessment' and realised that 'safety marshals' would need to be deployed at two strategic points. If a vehicle appeared the

Roller Skates of the day

shout of car, or bus, would be heard and a quick move onto the grass verge, or into the ditch, would be executed. Mind you back then the traffic was usually very light when compared to the present. However the 416 bus that ran from Leatherhead to Esher, did stop on one occasion and the conductor issued 'instructions' to us in an irate fashion. He told us that he would go in to the 'cop shop' and tell the Desk Sergeant what our game was. That last snippet of information was enough to make us terminate the practise. It went something like this. We did not want to be 'sorted out' by the local Constable, but worse than that our Fathers would be informed. No you don't even want to go there!

During the summer evenings, we would sometimes sit on the parapet of the Rye Brook Bridge and watch the traffic returning from the coast, we always referred to it as 'the seaside'. The coaches usually out numbered the cars and I can still name many of the companies, but I was and still am, something of an 'anorak'. Just to name

How many of you can remember a trip to the seaside in one of Bookham Saloon's coaches?

some: Southdown, Windsorian, Greygreen, Sutton Motors, Valliant, Royal Blue (yes they did do trips), Timpson's, Kingstonian, and many more, not forgetting Luff's and Law's. We also collected car numbers and wrote them down in our note books.

From the age of eleven or twelve some of us became interested in loco spotting (not train spotting please). For this activity we used to cycle to Esher, this being the nearest point on the main line. Suitably armed with our Ian Allan A.B.C. books listing every locomotive owned by and run on the rails of British Railways Southern Region, together with a bottle of Tizer and a buttered roll, we were all set for a day of excitement and anticipation. The object of the exercise was to 'bag' every loco in each class, an impossible task when you consider that the engines were 'shedded' all over the South and Southwest of England. If the weather was fine and of course it usually was (coloured glasses), we would find our usual spot to the North of the railway, on the golf course opposite the Greyhound pub, just past the Scilly Isles. If it did come onto rain, or the sun became too hot, we would get a platform ticket for one old penny and go on to the station.

A day spent watching steam locomotives, thundering up and down might seem boring to some people, but I can assure you that the thrill of seeing the

34

Lord Nelson, King Arthur, West Country, Merchant Navy and Battle of Britain class engines, together with a host of 'lesser' types was the best experience we lads could imagine at that time. Standing on the station platform we would watch as the signals were 'pulled off' for the 'up main line' and then strain our eyes towards Walton-on-Thames and try to identify the locomotive. As the train thundered by, the ground would shake and our guesses would be confirmed right or wrong. After the train had passed a quietness would prevail and you would be left with bird sounds and that wonderful smell of smoke, steam and hot oil. If I could bottle and successfully market that smell I would be a 'millionaire'.

Quick, the 'down main' has just been 'pulled off'. Oh dear! It's just an electric express and as the roof boards proclaimed, it was bound for 'Pompey' and 'The Isle of Wight'.

In the twenty-first century things are completely different. The freedoms we once had are slowly being eroded. Try standing, or sitting, on a Station

During the time in question none of the buildings behind the cottages existed. The whole area between the cottages and the railway bridge was taken up by the allotment of the author's Grandad.

platform for a period of time, assuming you are able to buy a platform ticket, just for the innocent pleasure of watching, or photographing the trains. You are very likely to be approached by a 'jobs worth' asking what is the nature of your business and you will probably be asked to leave. It would appear that we are all potential terrorists.

I have mentioned that I spent time with my Grandad on his allotment. If you did not know the local area in days gone by, I am going to ask you to exercise your imagination and come with me onto the railway bridge. We will stand just above the entrance to Buffers Lane, and look towards Ashtead. There are no flats. The engineering company that preceded the flats is not there. The car repair workshop is not there, in fact there is no building of any sort in view until we see the old railway cottages, which had been built by the London and South Western Railway.

The whole of this area was taken up by my Grandad's allotment. He paid a small rent to the Southern Railway and later to British Railways, for this privilege.

Mr and Mrs Pamplin lived in the right hand cottage. She was a lovely lady who gave Grandad cups of tea and plied me with 'pop'. All the ground between the cottages and the railway bridge was my Grandad's allotment. In the top left hand corner of the allotment was a large crab apple tree, underneath which was Grandad's tool shed, yes, you have guessed, it was built out of railway sleepers. Every type of crop was grown in this garden, including tobacco. Purely for personal use you understand, and yes, it was legal. He would cure this in molasses and I can remember my Mum saying to him "If you keep smoking that stuff Dad you'll kill us all". Grandad would just reply "is that a fact?".

The grass paths that ran between the plots were kept short and tidy with the use of a small hand scythe. If they had been cut with a lawn mower they would not have looked any better. The secret was to have a sharp edge on the blade. Grandad would achieve this with the use of a whet stone and plenty of spit. The acid test would be for him to take a cigarette paper from his pocket and cut it cleanly with the blade. The exercise would conclude with the words "he'll do boy".

On the south side of the railway stood the roofless, dilapidated shell of the original railway terminus. It was built by the Epsom and Leatherhead Railway Company and stood gaunt and defiant and completely alone. The station was not operated by the Epsom and Leatherhead Railway because, on completion, the line between Epsom and Leatherhead was taken over and run jointly by The London and South Western Railway and the London Brighton and South Coast Railway. This arrangement was in operation until the Southern Railway was formed on 1st January 1923.

The electric trains thundered by towards Dorking or Guildford. Some would be expresses bound for 'Pompey' or Bognor. Watching these trains passing by was a sheer delight to a small boy. The railway 'bug' is still with me.

At the age of eight I joined the cubs. My first cub pack was attached to the 5th Leatherhead (All Saints) Scout Group and we met in the All Saints Church Hall, which at the time was right by the railway bridge and until recently was

A recent view of the old All Saints Church Hall.

occupied by the Gardeners Benevolent Society. The Church Hall was then the centre of the known universe, hosting socials, whist drives, school plays, including serving as a classroom. I have this last snippet of information from friends who went to All Saints School. Remember my schooling, prior to the age of eleven, was spent 'Over the Bridge' at Fetcham.

I later joined the 1st Fetcham cubs because most of my school friends went there. At the age of eleven I went to the 1st Leatherhead Scouts, who met in Queen Ann's Terrace. I remained an active member of that group for over twenty years.

Shortly after the war a craze called 'cycle speedway' sprang up. It originated on the London bomb sites. An oval track would be marked out with bricks measuring approximately sixty feet by thirty feet. (At this distance in time these dimensions might not be correct, but you get the idea). Four riders would line up on the starting line and complete four or six laps. The surface lent itself to the execution of slides at the corners, just like motorcycle speedway.

This phenomena looked as though it could run for a long time and Phillips Cycles produced a speedway bike complete with the wide handlebars, curved crossbar and a large rear sprocket, producing a very low gear.

Not to be out done we had our own cycle speedway track. Initially this was located on an area of waste ground at the top end of Woodbridge Avenue and Sandes Place. The date would be c1952/3. Of course none of us could

A recent view of the bridge taken from the front of the old All Saint's Church Hall.

afford to purchase a Phillips speedway bike. We set about making our own from bits and pieces scrounged from the back of sheds and, yes, literally from under hedges and 'fished' out of various watery places. It provided us with hours of intense activity, bending handlebars out into a wide and flat configuration, building up bottom brackets, a task requiring patience and not an insignificant amount of dexterity. We also set steering head bearings. We had heavy duty grease everywhere and ball bearings all over the floor! The finished articles, once painted in any colour that was to hand, served their purpose well. Of course if I said that every creation was 'fit for purpose' I would be guilty of a terminological inexactitude. Finding suitable crash helmets was the most difficult part of the equation and needless to say, we did without them. I am pleased to report that I can't recall any of us sustaining serious injuries.

We had to find a name for our team because we would be competing in a local league that included teams from such exotic places as Fetcham and Bookham. For a short while we changed our venue to a patch of ground adjacent to the football ground and we called ourselves 'The Fetcham Grove Eagles'.

The name Eagle was taken from the Eagle comic which back then was reading material not to be missed by any self respecting lad. How many of us can still remember Dan Dare and the Mekons? If I remember correctly it was my old mate Goff who came up with this 'brain wave'. Not long after we had started this venture we got ourselves a manager, yes it was all becoming serious. We eventually moved to a piece of ground on the Kingston Road recreation ground where the youth club now stands and changed our name for the last time to 'The Leatherhead Eagles'. Our crowning glory was to take part in the Coronation parade with our bikes draped in copious quantities of red, white and blue ribbon.

A Fetcham Grove Eagles Programme

Just in case some of you thought I may have forgotten, we spent a considerable time playing 'Cowboys and Indians'. Back then in those 'politically incorrect' times

the girls had to be squaws and if I remember correctly spent some of the time tied to trees. One such squaw suffered this fate. The cowboys went home for their lunch (or dinner as it was then). After dinner they went round to call for said squaw. It was then they realised that she was still tied to the tree. I must tell you that this heinous crime took place 'Over the Bridge', but on the South side. The woods in question were those located behind the Leatherhead Hospital. They were much larger then. I know that this story is true because I married that squaw.

I have said previously that we had such freedom and were not constrained by some of the present day 'hang ups'. Muddy trousers, dirty knees, wet shoes, and indeed wet

What a happy patriotic lot we were. The Coronation street party in Woodbridge Grove. June 1953. The Revd Jonathan Edwards can be seen at the head of the table.

wellies (inside and out) seemed to be par for the course, we had all the 'street cred' you could want.

My ramblings cannot be allowed to pass without mentioning 2nd June 1953 the day Her Majesty Queen Elizabeth was crowned. The whole country went wild (in a truly British way you understand). Almost every street or estate, had a street party. Chairs and tables were commandeered from homes, village halls, schools and a host of other 'suppliers'. Our party took place in Woodbridge Grove. Flags and bunting were draped from the lamp posts, sides of houses and other suitable fixings. (there were still very few telegraph poles on the estate, just as well.)

Gramophones and sundry musical instruments were taken into the street. The tables groaned with goodies and remember that some food rationing was still in force. Mum's from up and down the road must have stocked up for the feast. Possibly another case of funny tummies at some stage of the proceedings.

At the time of the Coronation some of the Chelsea Pensioners were still billeted at the Leatherhead School for the Blind and they were a frequent sight in the town and surrounding areas. During the winter they wore their dark tunics, but during the summer they wore smart scarlet uniforms and some of them would make a brigade of guards look improperly dressed. (Of course I jest, most guardsmen are bigger than me, but you get the idea).

Two of these gentlemen were invited to our party and one of them in particular stays in my mind. He sported a fine moustache and carried a walking stick that was decorated with the red, white, and blue. He stayed in the town until all the Pensioners were 'returned to barracks' at the Royal Hospital in Chelsea and was always seen carrying his patriotic symbol.

Later in the afternoon Goff Powell and I put on a Punch and Judy show for the younger children. This led to us getting bookings to attend at other venues long after the Coronation celebrations had finished, but that, as they say is another story.

Another happy recollection from the late 1940's and early 1950's was the visit to the Kingston Road recreation ground of Lord 'George' Sanger's Circus. The erection of the big top accompanied by the clowns, animals and gaily coloured vehicles was a sight to behold. The

Two grand gentlemen, guests at the Woodbridge Grove Coronation party, June 1953. What a pity that this is not a coloured photograph. Their bright scarlet tunics had the ability to brighten even the darkest day. Some of the older pensioner's would have served in Queen Victoria's reign.

sense of excitement and wonder created by the arrival of the circus is difficult to imagine in today's world of instant entertainment.

It was a hands on activity and if one felt the need it was possible to have a go at bare back riding. You would be fitted with a harness and the horse would walk round

LORD JOHN SANGERS
VICTORY CIRCUS AND MENAGERIE
PROGRAMME
c1948

Performers:

- Pierrot & Pierrette
- Silly Sammy in Airborne Antics
- Nelson, Gymnast
- Bourget - Mirthful Genius
- Nigger - Wonder Pony
- Dante Shows His Paces
- Evelyn's Dogs and Pigeons
- Speedy and his Brains Trust Horse
- Little Drops of Water - One Huge Scream
- Andersons - Amazing Stilt Walkers
- Emeline on the Invisible Wire
- Domino - High School Horses
- Daredevil Ansons on the Lofty Wires

the circus ring while you tried to stand up on his back. Easier said than done. However I do know one young lady who tried her luck with a certain amount of success. She now goes by the name of Mrs Hennegan.

I can clearly remember the circular imprint of the circus ring that remained in the ground for months after the circus had left town.

With all this activity I begin to wonder how on earth we found time to go to school. Will such childhoods be attainable in the future? Who can tell. Do I hear the cry of 'rose tinted glasses' once more?

Chapter 5

Visiting Tradesmen and Mobile Shops

Today the concept of 'on line' shopping is catching on in a big way and is deemed to be a wonderful new concept. Of course the technology is something that could not have been imagined in the 1940's and 1950's. However you could request a home delivery service, albeit you had to 'phone, or take your order book into the shop. The goods would then be delivered to your door should you so wish.

As a result many delivery vehicles could be seen up and down the streets. I will describe just some of the trades people who were a frequent sight then.

The delivery service that probably made the most lasting impression on me was that of Ren's Bakery. They were the predecessor of Harrington's in Bridge Street, now alas, no longer in business. They had a horse drawn van which was painted grey. On each side of the van there was hand painted art work depicting a boy and girl climbing a staircase formed of cottage loaves. The staircase was in the shape of a pyramid and the boy and girl were approaching the 'summit' from opposite sides. The name of Ren's Bakery was prominent, together with a message alluding to health, but I regret I cannot recall what it said. (If any reader can remember I would by delighted to hear from them). Over subsequent years the business changed hands, becoming Morgan's, Holmes, and lastly, fondly remembered Harrington's.

The delivery man was Mr Booth. He would stop at the junction of Woodbridge Grove and Rye Brook Road. There he would tie his horse to the lamp post and fit the feeding bag to the horse. He would then fill an enormous basket with loaves, tuck his arm through the handle, and go from house to house with his customer's orders. Meanwhile the horse would be making short work of his feed. The ground would usually be covered with a variety of birds who no doubt regarded the dropped feed as their equivalent of a 'take-away'. Mind you back then we would not have known the term 'take-away', we knew it by another name i.e. 'the chippy'.

Another regular caller was Mr Downer, yes, the proprietor of the shop on the 'Plough' roundabout, which only recently ceased trading. He had a large green vehicle and carried almost every consumable item required by the housewife and indeed some items that could be needed by the man of the house. Let me mention some of these: washing lines, proper hemp not plastic, Ricketts

Blue, essential for getting those whites 'whiter than white', soap, including large blocks of Fairy Carbolic, I still love that smell, how could anything remain dirty after a good old scrub with that! Cold water dyes, ideal for a lady wishing to obtain a 'new' blouse together with scrubbing brushes, certain items of ironmongery, enamel bowls and jugs, small screws and nails, not in a packet but, "how many would you like sir?"

However the thing that always intrigued me was the way Mr Downer used to dispense paraffin. Suspended under the van was a tank of paraffin which had a large brass tap. If you required this commodity you took your can, or other suitable container along and asked for it to be filled up. Mr Downer would perform the task and you would pass over the required payment. Again I can't see this operation being allowed today. The Health and Safety Police would have confiscated his van and taken him to an appropriate place so that he could explain why such a hazardous and potentially dangerous operation was being performed in front of the general public and worse than that, in front of children. I expect Mr Downer's defence would be "they are not members of the general public, they are my customers".

A horse drawn milk float

Milk was another item to be delivered. Yes I know that this service is still available today but we had a milk float that was horse drawn. Mr Amos delivered milk for Prewetts Dairy, alas another old Leatherhead business that has gone the way of all flesh. The horse was an important member of Mr Amos' team. I expect he knew the round as well as Mr Amos, who would load himself up with two metal hand crates full of pint bottles and proceed to call on his customers. Whilst he was doing this his horse would keep up with him, adopting a slow walk and stopping when Mr Amos needed to replenish the crates. They have still not devised a delivery vehicle that can perform that feat. All the horses received attention from us kids. I still remember how tolerant and docile they were, although at times the delivery man would say to us "don't make a fuss of him today something has upset him". These episodes did not usually last long and next day the horse would be nudging you in the back in a playful manner.

Alas one day Mr Amos appeared with an electrical hand drawn float. The price of progress, I remember he told my Grandad it was a pain because he had to keep going back and forth to refill his crates. You see the electrical float didn't understand how the game was played and refused to move forward unaided when required to do so.

The Co-op also delivered both milk and bread. They used a tried and tested method of payment. My Mum would visit the Co-op shop (shades of Gracie Fields) for some of her provisions and whilst there she would purchase milk and bread tokens. These were metal, the milk tokens were triangular and the bread tokens were oval in shape (or was it the other way round). The requisite number of tokens would be left on the doorstep and the delivery man would collect them. Clever, no coins had to be left out, and the correct value was always available. Later on the tokens moved into the modern world and were made from plastic. They say people can always remember their Service Number and their Co-op Dividend (divi) Number. Mum's was 19981.

We also had our version of Steptoe and Son. Rag a' bone Joe would appear from time to time, ringing his bell, and calling "ra bo ra bo", at least I think that was what it was. It was always a mystery to us. I know at times we would follow on behind imitating him, but always vigilant in case he jumped off the cart in order to 'reason' with us.

Another eagerly awaited arrival was Raymond's ice cream van. He came from the Surbiton area and dispensed his wares from a magnificent red and cream coach built van The vehicle was based on a Morris commercial chassis. I can remember this because I thought at the time it was the name of the van. The ice cream was delicious, and even in our early stage of development us lads thought that his dark haired daughter was rather lovely.

Some times the street would be visited by the knife sharpening man. He arrived on the scene pushing a very complicated type of wheel-barrow. When someone wanted knives, garden shears, axes, or other items sharpened he would 'unfold' his wheel-barrow and as if by magic it transformed into a pedal driven sharpening device. He sat on a wooden bench seat and peddled in a brisk and business like manner driving the grind stone and producing a shower of sparks as he sharpened the implements.

The Muffin Man was also a visitor to our street, carrying his wares on a tray, more often than not perched on his head, and ringing a hand bell. He would turn up at weekends usually in time for tea. These would be toasted in front of the open fire and if you have not had the opportunity to sample freshly toasted crumpets soaked in margarine I can only sympathise with you. I feel sure that the open fire was the secret to the exquisite taste.

We were well served with ingredients for a gourmet meal because it was not only the Muffin Man that bought delights to the door. The Winkle man would arrive on Sundays. These culinary delights would be purchased by the pint. The measure was gathered from his container in an enamel pint mug and tipped into a paper bag. I can well remember the dexterity that was required to hook the winkles out of their shells. The black cap that enclosed the winkle would be placed on the side of your plate.

At first I did not care to try them but the adults played a game whereby they would place these caps round the edge of their plates counting them saying Monday, Tuesday, Wednesday, Thursday, Friday, Saturday, Mackintosh. I can't for the life of me recall how the game was played, or if and how any points were scored, but I was determined not to be left out so duly had my portion and still enjoy winkles, cockles and whelks. Perhaps my love of cockles is down to the fact that I was born just a 'stones throw' from Leigh-on-Sea in Essex.

Chapter 6

Transport

Despite any assumptions to the contrary, back in those distant days people did travel more than five miles radius from their homes. I jest, because most of our fathers had travelled into many corners of the world and all the travel costs had been paid for by no lesser a person than his Majesty the King. Indeed Dad had visited such exotic places as Africa and Italy including Catterick Camp in Yorkshire. It was not an adventure that any of them would have undertaken by choice and sadly many dads did not return. Our travel adventures were not as exciting or demanding, we made our journeys to places much nearer to home.

Where could one go to? For those of you who take an interest in such things let us look at the service provided by the buses in the area. In the 1940's, 1950's and 1960's Leatherhead and the surrounding area was served by a comprehensive bus service. In addition to the 462, already mentioned, the following services operated during the 1940's,1950's and 1960's.

The 65 route ran between Ealing Argyle Road and Leatherhead. This was a red bus, operated by London Transport Central Area, that wormed its way well into the green London Transport Country Area. When it travelled towards Leatherhead from Ealing it had a multitude of termination places, e.g. The Fox and Hounds at Malden Rushett, (now the Shy Horse), The White Hart at Hook, Copt Gilders at Chessington, not forgetting the Zoo. I can remember as a youngster waiting at Kingston with Mum for the Leatherhead bus and

I have a feeling that this photo was taken in the early post war period and shows a 65 close to the entrance to Pachesham Park gates, bound for Leatherhead Bus Garage. It was obviously high summer as every possible window is open. Note the Driver's white uniform jacket. There! I am proven right, the sun did always shine when we were young.

having to read all these destinations. If you were lucky the first 65 would be yours.

On other occasions all the destinations would appear before the Leatherhead bus turned up. In those far off days it was a common occurrence for bus routes to terminate in a pub forecourt.

The 93 ran from Putney to Dorking. This was another red bus. It only terminated at Dorking during the summer months thus enabling the 'South Londoners' to visit Box Hill and other local beauty spots.

Then there was the 408 Guildford to Croydon with some journeys to Warlingham.

416	Leatherhead	to	Esher
418	Epsom	to	Bookham
470	Dorking	to	Croydon

In addition to these services Leatherhead had three Green Line coaches passing through.

712	Dorking	to	Luton
713	Dorking	to	Dunstable
714	Dorking	to	Luton

(the 714 took a different route south and north of London)

Most Green Line coaches passed through London. Many going via Victoria. The Green Lines worked on a limited stop system and you could only board or alight at dedicated stops. There was also a minimum fare, so those persons who only wished to go a short distance were discouraged from doing so and would wait for their normal service bus. Just after the war and up to the early 1950's the Green Line services were, in the main, operated by the TF type coaches. Some readers might remember them.

They were distinctive vehicles with under floor engines and the radiator was formed by a downward curve just under the nearside front window. It was the seat behind this window that was the best in 'the

The TF Type Green Line coach. The seat in the front just foreword of the sliding entrance door was the one to make for.

47

house' but usually some miserable person who had boarded before Leatherhead would be firmly in possession and you had to hope that they were not going as far you. When this seat was vacated a fast manoeuvre was required. If successful we were there until we got to London, we never travelled on the route north of the capital. In later years I did take journeys north of London, but by then the RF type vehicles were in use.

We have now seen the demise of the Green Line coach with their distinctive roof route boards. On the bright side, there are now comprehensive coach services serving much of the country and providing a comparatively cheap method of transportation.

I realise that we are venturing a little way from 'The Bridge', but the following activity might be of interest.

During Derby Week the bus came into its own. There was a need to get the punters from Epsom Railway Station to the Downs. This miracle of mass transportation was provided by the ever faithful bus. A Marquee would appear in Epsom Station forecourt. This was the operational nerve centre and 'feeding' area for the crews. Remember there were two crew members per bus in those good old days, i.e. a driver and a conductor.

The buses would form a continuous 'conveyer belt' between the Station and the Downs. When one bus was full the Inspector would wave it off and the next one would load up. Each double decker would carry approximately 60 people including the 'standees'. The operation would be reversed when the race meeting ended.

With an increased car ownership this practice gradually declined, but even today, during Derby Week, the south coast is rather deprived of its open top double deckers.

The railways provided employment for many members of my Mother's family and she has been heard to say that "the Watt's and the Kemp's ran the Railways" - a gross exaggeration but you get the drift.

I would go to Leatherhead Railway Station for one of two reasons. Either to accompany my Grandfather to his office, which at the time was located on the 'down' platform of the old disused London and South Western Railway, or to travel by train. Grandad's office was, to my young eyes, a very grand affair consisting of a large desk and a Windsor back chair. The office was heated by a turtleback stove and if you took the round lid off on the top, the kettle would cover the space and boil faster than an atomic power station. Not that any of us knew what an atomic power station was. That was years into the future.

Back to 'The Bridge'. When I accompanied Grandad to the railway station we did not walk all along Kingston Road and up Randalls Road to get to the station, like the ordinary folk did. On the south side of the bridge, where the industrial estate in now located, was the Railway Goods Yard. The sidings came almost to the Kingston Road and contained four or five lines. Usually there was a large assortment of trucks and wagons on each of the lines.

When we got to the foot of the bridge we entered the yard through the large white gate that guarded the siding, together with prominent notices prohibiting lesser mortals than me and Grandad from entering the site.

I was not concerned in the least because I knew that my Grandad was a very important Railway Man. We would proceed along the line of trucks and wagons. I had to keep my eyes open and take care where I trod, (there were of course no 'live' rails in the yard but you could bump your head on buffers or coupling chains).

However when we reached the station area we had to cross the electrified lines to get to the office on the old station and of course we had to cross the 'live' lines. This must be done with care. I had been continually schooled about the danger of the 'live' line, the ones that contained the juice. "Touch that boy and you'll jump very high". I knew the danger. Grandad had shown me a large scar on the inside of his right arm. When he was a young platelayer he was working on the line in the Clapham Junction area. He had dropped a tool that lay on the ground between the 'live rail' and the 'running rail'. Instead of reaching for it under the rails he put his hand between the two rails and caught his arm on the live rail. He told me, "I should be building a railway line for St Peter", but as the incident took place during the height of summer the ground was dry and fortunately he was standing on a wooden sleeper.

The Southern Railway had plans to build a line from Motspur Park to Leatherhead. Prior to the outbreak of war in 1939 the line had been completed as far as Chessington South. Work then stopped. However, after the war work did recommence and a swathe of ground was cleared through the Ashtead Woods. The sound of tree roots being blasted would occasionally break the silence. If you take a stroll through the woods it is still possible to locate the remaining concrete fence posts that mark the intended course of the line. Just before you get to The Star Public House at Malden Rushett, it is possible to find two large section concrete posts marking the position of the intended accommodation crossing that would have served one of the tracks that ran from there to Ashtead.

Behind the houses in Clare Cresent a curved fence line can still be seen indicating the intended course of the track.

I can still remember going with Grandad to see the new bridge that crossed over Chalky Lane, opposite Chessington Zoo (now The World of Adventures). A locomotive was being run over the bridge. I now know that deflection tests were being carried out, but back then all I knew was that the whole thing was very exciting.

As a piece of useless information, two routes between Leatherhead and Motspur Park, would have been almost the same distance, a difference of only a few chains.

Shortly after this brief resumption of work the plans to complete the line were dropped, due to increasing costs, the pending nationalisation from 1st January 1948 and 'green belt' legislation.

There were other forms of transport in my life. When Dad returned from the war he began to settle back into life in 'civvy street' and wanted to be independent as far as transport was concerned. He was working for the Liverpool and Victoria Insurance Society, (or the 'Liverpool Vic' as it was and still is known), this involved an amount of travelling. His office was based at Redhill but his duties took him all around the Dorking, Reigate and Burgh Heath area and more besides. What better means of transport to perform this task than a motorbike.

Dad had many motorbikes, Royal Enfield, B.S.A. and more, but the one that I remember best was the 500cc Norton. I travelled many miles on the box shaped pillion, as indeed did Mum. I remember helping Dad when the engine needed a 'de-coke', at least I think that was what I was doing. We would finish up with various parts spread out on a clean sheet all around us. Needless to say, they were all returned to their proper place. Dad would have an expression of relief on his face when, with a hefty jump on the kick start the monster was brought roaring back into life? I can still hear Mum saying, "Eric you haven't got that bike in bits again?"

I had uncles and aunts living in Hounslow and Pinner. Dad and I would ride over to see one or the other of them on a Sunday. Whether Dad really wished to see them or he used it as an excuse for a trip out, I am not sure. Looking back on these excursions I often wonder if they said "Oh lord it's Eric again".

However I caught the motorbike 'bug' which is still with me. Ros and I put many miles in on our BMW Sidecar outfit. My excuse, "it keeps us young". Though in the winter it is a little cold, but I am sure it beats swimming in the Serpentine on Christmas Day!

Later Dad had a variety of cars. The first was a 1937 Austin Cambridge, which transported us on many a trip. Two in particular spring to mind. A visit to Wells and Cheddar Caves, and a run to Brighton when one of the front spring leaves worked loose. This resulted in a slow return home with a distinct list to port. This was followed by a 1946 Hillman Minx with a soft top. Although it was a

The Austin A40

lovely car Mum thought it was not very practical, so it had to go. Dad, of course, was adamant that the 'executive decision ' was his alone.

An Austin A40 then joined the family. I thought this car was the finest thing on four wheels. Perhaps I was influenced by the fact that I learnt to drive in it.

I can still remember my very first outing, negotiating Surbiton High Street under the watchful eye of Mr Collinson and arriving back home with all the paint work in place and no dents! I am pleased to say that shortly after that I took my test at Surbiton and passed first time. (Sorry I am bragging and that is not worthy of me, ah well!).

Chapter 7
Schooling for the Big Boys

My period in secondary education involved being on both sides of The Bridge. Before the days of Therfield, Leatherhead County Secondary School was on the site now occupied by Trinity School.

Stanley Arthur Moore, Headmaster of Leatherhead County Secondary School with some of the Senior Girls in the 1950's

The Headmaster was Mr Stanley Arthur Moore, known by everyone as 'Sam', but never within ear-shot you understand. I remember he had a rather unique way of dealing with bullying. He threatened to put the culprit into the boxing ring with one of the pupils, who was a local boxing champion. I don't remember any significant problems in that area, and be under no illusion, 'Sam' would have exercised the deterrent.

All the pupils from Leatherhead, Ashtead, Fetcham and Bookham who had not passed the eleven plus examination were sent to the Secondary School. (All the brainy ones went mainly to Dorking Grammar, or Rosebery at Epsom).

We were all streamed, in the parlance of the day, into five grades namely A,B,C,D,E. The education was, in my opinion, sound, and was in the vanguard of its time. As an example, the girls did Domestic Science, this entailed among other things learning to cook. I read in the media that this idea seems to be favoured by some of the 'experts' and they want to reintroduce cooking into the school curriculum. Well, I'll go to the foot of our stairs!

The boys did Carpentry and Metal work, both sexes did Maths, English, Science, Art, Religious Study, Music, French, Geography, and oh yes!

Leatherhead County Secondary School

Forgive the self indulgence. This picture shows the author's mother with her class, after All Saint's School had moved 'Over the Bridge' into the 'small school' building vacated by Leatherhead County Secondary School.

another 'advanced idea', we all did PT. With the girls under Miss Owen and the boys under Mr Lane, I don't think many of us were obese.

Although I was never a lot of use on the football field, I do have fond memories spending wet days in the canteen with 'Stan' Lane outlining play tactics on a blackboard. Imploring us to consider "what would Matthews do"? He was of course referring to the great Stanley Matthews, later Sir Stanley. Even I, being a Philistine, knew who he was.

This was before all the school playing fields had been sold off and yes, there were winners and losers, although if you were not too far behind you might be referred to as a runner-up. Did I hear that some more 'experts' now think that competitive games could be worth a try?

At this time the school playing fields were situated at the top of Dilston Road where Therfield School now stands, The 'changing rooms' were located in an old and rather dilapidated Nissen Hut. No showers, not even any running water, still the mud would harden and could be scraped off during the maths lesson. Never mind it made us into the men and women we became!

New School Badge

In 1953 some of the classes began to transfer to the new school in Dilston Road. At this time the school buildings consisted of the main entrance hall, the canteen, the main assembly hall, together with the classrooms to the left of the corridor and two science labs at the far end of the corridor. The toilets were on the right hand side of the corridor.

Upstairs, the 'small hall' over the main entrance was the music room and the class rooms replicated those on the ground floor.

The showers were to the left and behind the assembly hall, as one faced the stage. There were strictly 'girl and boy' facilities. You only had to experience the 'flick' of a towel on a wet backside administered by the PT master to know your place. Remember, back then, to most of us the shower facility was a completely new experience.

The erection of the ROSLA (Raising Of School Leaving Age) building and extension of the main building did not take place until long after my contemporaries and I had gone out into the big wide world.

I think that we all found the new buildings much brighter than those 'Over The Bridge' in Kingston Road. They still had the smell of 'newness' for quite some time after we had taken up residence. It was strictly 'plimsolls only' in the main assembly hall and if you had forgotten to bring them then socks were the order of the day and woe betide anyone who went round the corners whilst placing a 'grubby mitt' on an adjacent pillar.

Chapter 8

All Change

In 1953 I sat the entrance exam at Vickers Armstrongs, Weybridge, to see whether I would 'cut the mustard' and be accepted as a trade apprentice in their Tool Room. If you were not cut out to be a Mathematician, or a Brain Surgeon, then at that time an apprenticeship with Vickers ran a very close second. I very soon learnt that the Tool Makers thought that they were a cut above the rest, a sentiment with which I wholeheartedly agree, there I go bragging again!

The examiner must have been rather sleepy on the day of the exam because I passed and so began some of the most enjoyable years of my working life. I still recall, with fond affection, being taken through the assembly hall and seeing the Valiant Bombers being built and thinking 'wow and they are going to pay me as well'.

The Vickers Valiant. The first of the V Bombers. Wow! And they are also going to pay me.

In 1956 the family moved 'Over the Bridge' to Newton Wood Road in Ashtead. I lived there for five years until I got married, when I moved back to Leatherhead. I can now be on the bridge in two and a half minutes and still walk and drive over it often.

As I said in my opening remarks, memory is a funny thing. It can be very selective. It can be manipulated to comply with the aspirations of the individual in question, rather like a minute secretary who records what he or she had wished they had heard and not what was actually said. I have to confess that I have been guilty of this myself, but I hope that my memories recorded here do not fall into that category.

How soon today becomes yesterday. Count the number of times we have said "no, was it as long ago as that?". It is true, the older we get the quicker time goes by. I have a theory as to why this should be the case. When we were ten years old five years was half of our lifetime. When we are sixty years old five years is one twelfth of our life. Well that is my story and I'm sticking to it.

History is determined by those who have written it.

Today is tomorrow's history.

'Gosh' was it as long ago as that?

PUBLICATIONS

The Society has published or compiled a number of books on the local history of the area and the following are presently available:-

A History of Ashtead, edited by Jack Stuttard, 1995	£ 9.99
History of Fetcham, edited by Jack Stuttard, 1998	£ 8.95
Bookham in the Twentieth Century, by Bill Culley, 2000	£ 6.50
History of Headley, edited by Jack Stuttard, 2001	£ 7.95
Archive Photographs Series – Leatherhead, compiled by Linda Heath, 1996	£12.99
Leatherhead and District. Then and Now, compiled by Linda Heath and Peter Tarplee, 2005.	£12.99
Leatherhead, A History, by Edwina Vardey, 2001	£15.99
The Swan Leatherhead and its Brewery, by Mary Rice-Oxley, 2001	£ 5.95
The Inns and Public Houses of Leatherhead and District, by Goff Powell. 2006	£ 5.50

Copies may be ordered from the Sales Secretary, L&DLHS, at the address detailed below. Cheques should be made payable to 'L&DLHS' and p&p is free.

Other books of local interest may be purchased from the Leatherhead Museum.

For information regarding Museum opening hours, Membership, and Lectures contact Leatherhead & District Local History Society, Leatherhead Museum Hampton Cottage, 64 Church Street LEATHERHEAD Surrey KT22 8DP

Tel: 01372 386348

Leatherheadmuseum@localhistory.free-online.co.uk

Web site: www.leatherheadlocalhistory.org.uk